I0488044

The Magic...

*Optimize **Business Success,
Relationships** & **Life** Through
My Lessons Learned*

Rick Munson

Published by Rick Munson.

For corrections, company/title updates, comments, or any other inquiries, please e-mail Rick.Munson@msisolutions.com

First Printing, 2019
10 9 8 7 6 5 4 3 2 1

ISBN number 978-0-359-87272-5

Copyright © 2019 by Rick Munson. All rights reserved. Printed in the United States of America. No part of this publication may be reproduced or distributed in any form or by any means, or stored in a database or retrieval system, except as permitted under Sections 107 or 108 of the U.S. Copyright Act, without prior written permission of the publisher. This book is printed on acid-free paper.

Material in this book is for educational purposes only. This book is sold with the understanding that neither the author nor the publisher is engaged in rendering legal, accounting, investment, or any other professional service. Neither the publisher nor the author assumes any liability for any errors or omissions, or for how this book or its contents are used or interpreted, or for any consequences resulting directly or indirectly from the use of this book. For legal advice or any other, please consult your personal lawyer or the appropriate professional.

Groups may order copies of the book at a group discount by contacting Rick Munson at rick.munson@msisolutions.com .

Throughout this book, the Cambria type font was used for headlines, and text was set using the Calibri font.

The views expressed by the individuals in this book do not necessarily reflect the views shared by the companies they are employed by (or the companies mentioned in) this book. The employment status and affiliations of the author with the companies referenced are subject to change.

Contents

PROLOGUE 4

The Magic and Miracle 5

Family, the first days...7

Early Life Lessons 9

The Power of Education 11

Military Leadership, the Experience............................ 13

Military and Leadership Learned 18

Ninety Percent of Life is Just Showing Up................... 23

Gaining Business Experience 26

Entrepreneur Keys which Start your Business.............. 30

The Power of Relationships 33

Life's Daring Adventure as a Risk Taker 37

Growing the Business.. 40

The Balance of Business and Family............................ 43

The Business Planning Process................................... 46

Goals, Budgets and Reviews...................................... 48

Reflections for your success....................................... 51

Epilogue 74

Appendix... 75

About the Author.. 87

PROLOGUE

While serving as an entrepreneur mentor at Arizona State University in 2018, I will never forget one of my students' questions: "Rick, how in the world did you find time to successfully take care of your family, while at the same time successfully grow and take care of your companies? How did you successfully balance your time, focus and energy?" These questions have now been asked of me many times and is the foundation and the spirit from which I created this leadership guide.

This book contains my key lessons learned on how to create scalability and sustainability into your company, focus on positivity and a balanced life, all while taking good care of your family. The power of my "Five 'A's" including Awareness, Acceptance, Action, Allowance, and Attitude in building corporate culture and a loving family life are one of the major KEY's you will learn in this book.

Following all the experiences you'll read about, and after leading a very healthy, prosperous life filled with positive energy, I was shocked and in fear when diagnosed with a rare form of stage four cancer in 2017. It was a tough battle of chemo and daily radiation treatments which did nothing at first but land me in the hospital with a serious illness and a horrible case of C-Diff.

After struggling through these illnesses and much hospital time healing, I was back on the chemo and radiation treatments for several months. All this time, I felt miserable as I had no taste, no appetite and worst of all, no energy. Finally, a Pet Scan, and my doctor declared me "Cancer Free". My next year was filled with travel and fun with my family. Then, in 2019, another Scan showed the cancer in my tumor had returned. The following "business, family, and life lessons learned helped me fight this next stage of cancer attacking my entire body and was my inspiration to write this book.

Chapter One

The Magic and Miracle

It was 3:30pm on a Tuesday afternoon at my company, Multi-Systems, Inc (MSI) in Phoenix, Az. I found myself, as usual on Tuesday and Thursday afternoons, rushing to check out with the MSI team. At MSI I was the founder and CEO to over 200 employees. We were responsible for developing the technology and installing then supporting complex computer systems for over 6000 hotels throughout North America. As hotels are open 24 hours per day, so was MSI. However, I had learned my lessons over the years and was placing my family first. As the MSI team all knew, on these Tuesday and Thursday afternoons, I was off to coach my three sons and their sport teams on the soccer fields, basketball courts, baseball diamonds or football fields depending on the time of year.

I loved leading MSI as CEO. At the same time, I loved being a dad and coaching youth sports. I was very blessed to have learned over the years, through many trials, tribulations and experiences, the keys to finding peace, happiness and joy while successfully raising a family and growing a business. I also discovered I was learning as much from my three sons and their soccer friends as I was from my employees and customers. The magic and miracle were finding this life balance and sharing my lessons learned from being a dad, raising three sons, and coaching youth sports while taking care of my and

MSI team and their families. The purpose of this book is to share these experiences and lessons learned for all entrepreneurs who wish to raise a family and grow a company while experiencing personal happiness and success in life.

Chapter Two

Family, the first days

First, it helps to know my beginnings. I was born and raised in a modest two story, three-bedroom, one-bathroom home planted in the small Dutch town of Holland, Michigan. My family consisted of a feisty younger brother, "know all" older sister, a loving mom who treasured teaching first grade, a hard-working entrepreneur father who never seemed to be around and a snappy gray Schnauzer. Five miles from our home was beautiful Lake Michigan where, as a growing child, I learned to swim, ice skate, water ski, drive hydro planes, race sail boats and chase girls on the beach.

Today, I realize that my father, always traveling and not being available for his family, impacted me more than I realized. I found myself missing him and feeling lonely when he was not around to spend time with me. This was especially true at all my sporting and musical events. I found myself looking in the stands for him. Sometimes, I would find my mom, and she would smile and wave at me. All I could do was try to view my dad sitting next to my mom. These memories bring tears to my eyes as I write.

To bury these feelings, I immersed myself in school and many activities. That resulted in what I believe was a good thing. I became an over achiever and wanted to me a "better dad" when I grew older. I was one who took on as many activities as there was time in the day and determined to, at the same time, be the best at what I was doing.

My dad did find some time for me on occasional weekends. My favorite fun thing to do with him in the summer was to take a long walk on the beach from our Cottage on Lake Michigan to Ottawa Beach where he bought us vanilla Ice crème cones. This memory puts a warm and happy smile on my face. Our long walks taught me the power of spending "one on one" time with your dad.

To this day, I share with my friends and associates who ask me, "how have you managed to raise such three successful sons?" My answer is simple and has been repeated many times: Unconditional Love for them and personal "in the moment being present" TIME with them. I also consistently share the power in the book "The Five Love Languages' with my children and my friends. One of the Five love languages is "spending one on one time with your child". You will learn more about the Five Love Languages a little later in this book.

My father did teach me one more very important lesson as he patiently showed me how to tend the small flower beds we had at home and how to properly mow the grass. The lesson was "if you are going to do it, do it right". WOW, what a powerful piece of advice. One which I have practiced the rest of my life. Doing it right became a valuable subconscious driving principle and value to me through my younger years. Doing it right also became a very conscious value to me when I founded my first MSI, and while being CEO at MSI 2 and MSI 3 as you will learn later.

Chapter Three

Early Life Lessons

High School was busy, fun and always challenging for me as I played on the Holland High football, basketball and track teams, played saxophone in our school band, chased more girls, and was the founder and lead guitar player in a money-making rock band; The Castaways. Thinking back, I suppose you could label this my first successful "startup". You will soon learn about my future startups including MSI 1, 2 and 3.

Back to my high school days, I founded my band, created the name, selected four musician friends, organized practices, marketed the band, insured all of us and equipment arrived on time for our gigs, collected payment for our work and divvied up the cash to our band. I must admit, it was always fun making my first payrolls at the age of 16.

I also managed to find time for my first job working summers as a busboy at the Point Resort on Lake Macatawa. There, I began learning how to be part of a team and be of service to our guests. Collaboration was the lesson being experienced. Of course, I still found time for my water sports on Lake Michigan and tanning on the white sand beaches with my friends. In the winters, we snow skied the "mostly white" slopes of Carousel Mountain next to the shores of Lake Michigan where we water skied in the summers. All this only five miles from our home.

My conscious High School years were fun and exciting. However, I did have my challenges. Trying to keep up with all my activities while dating and studying to get good grades which were ACCEPTABLE to my mom (the first-grade teacher) was always a challenge. At times I felt frustrated, lost and lonely. Subconsciously, I learned later, I was missing by dad who was busy flying around the world as Chief Financial Officer for Holland Furnace.

My lowest point during these years was when my father came home one day after a long trip. He shared with me and our family how he was just fired from his job and had no more work. Soon after, Holland Furnace declared bankruptcy which was a direct result from personal greed and a lack of good corporate governance at all Senior Levels.

My father was part of this complete corporate failure. I felt sad, scared and lonely, as I am sure my father felt also. I told myself I never wanted to be fired from a future job. I wanted to work for a company that nobody stole from and that had good, defined and practiced values. As discovered later in life, the only way to insure this was to build your own company.

Chapter Four

The Power of Education

In 1960, following my graduation from High School, I found myself off to the University of Wyoming in Laramie. Talk about "personal" disruption. The move took me from the sunny lakes and beaches of Michigan to the Wild West and rolling windy, cold plains of cowboy country. Why? I followed my BIG dreams of landing a spot on the Wyoming football team just as my sister's boyfriend had. Big first personal mistake! On the fields, I quickly discovered the "huge dudes" on football scholarships who were out there to crush, bruise and ridicule me. After picking myself up and licking my wounds, I threw my new Cowboy helmet in my life-lessons-learned ring.

It was then I decided it was best to focus on fraternities, drinking beer, chasing girls, working in the cafeteria, and my passion of snow skiing. Any time left over I would spend on my education. I also had to work to pay most of my way through college.

I was up at 5:30am most mornings reporting for work at the university cafeteria. I must have cracked enough eggs and opened enough cans of grape juice to feed Armies. After four wild and crazy years in Laramie, Wyoming (and many fun ski trips to Colorado), I managed to graduate UofW as a distinguished ROTC military graduate with degrees in business, finance and military science. As I learned later from a military recruiter's view, our CONTINUING EDUCATION is one of the top three "most important things we do in life". The other two will soon follow in my story.

On a personal note, while EXPERIENCING MY trials and tribulations of college, I dated my first wife Barbara. We "happenstance met" at the Denver airport where we both found ourselves stranded from a cancelled Frontier airlines flight to Laramie due to blizzards.

Life happens. After hopping a train to Cheyenne, Wyoming (which would bring us closer to Laramie) we soon discovered we were both from Michigan, 19 years old, and attending UofW. Barbara and I were married the summer of our graduation in Detroit, MI. She was a good partner who skied side by side with me down steep mountain slopes, loved to travel, party and race Hobby Cats with me on the Pacific Ocean. I learned later, she also happened to be a great salesperson.

Chapter Five

Military Leadership, the Experience

Following my marriage, I was proudly commissioned a Second Lieutenant in the Third Army Calvary Regiment, (3/3 ACR). The year was 1965 and my five years of military service followed. We soon found ourselves being shipped off to Fort Riley, Kansas for my officers training course. There, I found myself slinging a 45 Cal on my hip, running five miles at 5am every day, charging hills with 75-pound backpacks, learning how to jump out of perfectly good airplanes, and to "drink as an officer".

For the next four years I served as Lieutenant / Troop Executive Officer in the Third Armored Calvary regiment with platoon and troop leadership positions at Fort Lewis, (Seattle) Washington and Fort Bliss, (El Paso) Texas.

I learned how to command a battle tank, shoot it's 50 Cal machine gun and have my crew fire the tank's 155mm cannon at the same time. Most important, I learned how to be a successful Tank Platoon leader and lead a combat ready Cavalry Troop through hot and demanding deserts on live fire exercises.

After our three years training in Texas deserts, we were deemed combat ready to fight in "Desert Storm." My military leadership training and experiences were demanding, exciting, fear laden, and filled with the unexpected. The following details a few of the experiences and lessons learned.

In addition to my many military responsibilities as an Officer in the Calvary at Fort Bliss, I still found time to pursue my passion for snow skiing. As it turned out, in Ruidoso, New Mexico, 80 miles away from Fort Bliss, there was a beautiful and challenging ski area. A friend of mine, Pete Lilly, was a fellow Officer in the Cav who happened to be an awesome snow skier and skied on the Ruidoso Ski Patrol.

RELATIONSHIPS bring amazing opportunities and adventures to our lives. Pete encouraged me to try out for the Ski Patrol and much to my surprise and happiness I made the trials. What followed was a two-month intense EDUCATION on First Aid training and administering help and first aid on the hill. After many hours of practical exercises on the slopes, I passed the final ski test and exams. I received my prized maroon Professional Ski Association jacket with the big yellow medical cross on the back. I still have this jacket and prize it to this very day.

My leadership training was intense and filled with many cross-country moves. The first was my Officers Basic training course at Fort Riley in Wichita, Kansas and then on to Armor Basic Training at Fort Knox, Kentucky.

We then moved to Fort Benning GA for Air Born training and finally on to my first duty assignment at Fort Lewis, WA. After many months of training, trials, tests and travel, I was commissioned an Officer in the Third Armored Calvary Regiment: The Brave Rifles. We were based in Fort Lewis, WA with over 10,000 troops and their families.

As a Distinguished Military graduate from college, I had the honor to choose my branch and first duty station. I chose the 3/3 ACR and Fort Lewis, WA as I loved to snow ski and spend time on the water sailing. What a better place to do that than in Seattle, WA? There, the blue Pacific Ocean was only 30 minutes away and challenging ski slopes only a two-hour drive to the mountains. I would soon be training with our troops in the beautiful green Washington forests with the ocean as our backdrop. Thus, the dream, expectations and my vision anyway.

After the move to Fort Lewis we settled into our living quarters on Base. I was soon assigned to be a Tank Platoon Leader in the 3RD ACR. Being only 21 years old, fresh out of college and with limited Armor Officers basic training in Fort Knox Kentucky, I found myself in a very scary leadership position with many responsibilities. As a junior 2nd Lieutenant commanding a Tank Platoon, I was responsible to lead the enlisted men and Non-Commissioned Officers (NCO's) who had years of military EXPERIENCE as tank commanders and fighters. I also had to sign for and be responsible for five M60-A1 Main Battle Tanks along with all the equipment that went with them.

To add to my experience and relationships, I vividly remember my first field exercises at Fort Lewis. My tank platoon was deep in the North West forests where it was very cold with a never-ending freezing driving rain. The lead tank which I was also commanding threw a track in the middle of a deep gorge.

I soon found myself in the pouring rain, sticky cold mud and the dark of the night while helping my tank crew get our 2000-pound steel / rubber track back on our tank's sprockets. After successfully completing our task with much teamwork, the rest of that night was spent inside our tank with my crew. We were shivering and tried to stay warm from a lit Sterno Can placed on the breach block of our tank's 120 mm cannon.

This miserable experience taught me my Army lessons were going to be completely unexpected. More important, it helped me learn the importance that, as a LEADER, at times, we must "roll up our sleeves" and get dirty as we help our troops and employees accomplish a mission. Leadership by example was being taught to me through my experiences in the field.

The next day, I found myself in the bright sunshine, beautiful green forests, and surrounded by my tank platoon. The scene from my tank cupula gave me a whole new fresh and positive attitude. After moving out through the thick wet forests, our tank platoon soon came upon a clearing. There, in all its beauty, a snow-capped Mount Rainier appeared in the far distance. This sight I will never forget...hard to believe we were training for warfare with such beauty in the distance.

However, after my first six months at Fort Lewis, rumors began floating through the troops, that the entire Regiment, along with their families, were going to be deployed to Fort Bliss, Texas.

After being stationed at Fort Lewis for many years, the 3rd ACR and all their families had become accustomed to enjoying the beauty of the green forests and blue oceans of the North West. There was "shock and disbelief" that the unit was going to be deployed to the hot deserts surrounding Fort Bliss in El Paso, Texas. The Military had strategically determined that the next wars were going to be fought in the Mideast deserts over oil...and not in the forests defending Europe from Russian invasions. You can say the Army "moved our cheese."

We soon received new orders deploying the entire Regiment to the deserts of Fort Bliss, Texas. Our orders were to begin preparing for what was soon to become "Desert Storm" to be fought in the Mideast. I will never forget the challenge, hard work and determination it took to load all the Regiments more than 3000 tanks and vehicles onto rail cars and ship them off to Fort Bliss.

The even more challenging efforts were to keep the morale of our troops and families up as they mentally began to "ACCEPT" the realization that they would soon find their new homes in the deserts of El Paso. This EXPERIENCE was a good lesson for me in the importance of LISTENING and good COMMUNICATION when big disruption is happening in your company.

Change is good only if everyone on your team is AWARE, ACCEPTS and knows all the ACTIONS required to make change happen. Your team needs to share their ideas and be included in the planning process to make the disruptive change successful. This will help you, and everyone in your company, keep a positive ATTITUDE as your team travels down a new and sometimes very scary road which can find you and your team filled with fear

Chapter Six

Military and Leadership Learned

After a very successful move of our Unit to Fort Bliss, we soon settled in our new military quarters. All our equipment and tanks arrived safely soon after. Army green camouflage covered our uniforms and all our Tanks and Equipment as was required by our Calvary Regiment to be ready to fight in the forests of Europe. Our first mission was to desert camouflage all our tanks vehicles and uniforms, so we would blend into our brand-new hot desert surroundings.

In addition, soon after arriving at Fort Bliss, I was fortunate to be selected to participate in a new leadership training program the 3/3 ACR was offering to a few officers.

Continuing EDUCATION was becoming one of the most important things in my life and the Army was helping fill that desire. We experienced intense classes and lessons in how to "lead by listening". The Army was on a new trend. That was, to accomplish a successful mission as a leader, you must listen to and get ideas from your experienced NCO's and troops on the tactical options and best ways to carry out your strategic mission.

Having completed these courses I realized (and was frankly amazed) that the Army was changing their leadership process. The old way was for the Platoon Leader to tell his NCO's that "we are going to attack this town, here's how we are going to do it, and your marching orders are attached."

The new way was to share the mission (we need to attack this town) then LISTEN to tactically how the leadership team felt the best way to accomplish the mission was. That way, as a unit, we have collaborated, and the leadership team all agree on the timeline, people and resources needed to accomplish the strategic mission. I found out later in life that the same leadership principles worked miracles when starting my own companies.

After all our uniforms and equipment were camouflaged, and our "on base" training complete, we began our field training with weeklong exercises in the deserts surrounding Fort Bliss. It was miserable, as the desert was hot, dusty and unforgiving. The opposite of what we experienced in the forests of the North West.

Our vehicles soon began breaking down from the heat and dust and we were getting lost in the desert from the confusing terrain. Our previously proud 3/3 "Brave Rifles" Calvary Units were coming back to home base with only half their vehicles operational and the rest being towed and left or lost in the deserts.

Our troops, NCO's and officers all suffered through the confusion and extra work of our equipment constantly breaking down and getting lost in the desert. We were not even close to being combat ready. Following these experiences and my new leadership training, I informally sat down with my NCO team in our Motor Pool. As their Troop Executive Officer, I asked them, "what can we do to prevent all these equipment breakdowns in the desert?" As I explained, we are not even close to being ready to be deployed to fight a war in the

Mideast. This was especially true if half our equipment is going to break down even before we were engaged in combat.

My NCO's felt the root cause of all the breakdowns were two-fold. One, our troops were not taking proper care of their tanks on a "first level" basis. And second, most of the warning or "sending" units which alert our troops that their engine or vehicle was about to break down were not functional.

As a team, we agreed the solution was to pull every engine in our Unit, perform second level maintenance, and fix each and every sending unit. That would take care of the second part of our defined problem. The first part, motivating our troops to take better care of their equipment, was left to me. Another personal and very scary challenge as a young officer fresh out of college.

My company commander was not happy when he learned of our proposed solutions. I told him in my, and our NCO's collaborative opinion, to have the best Troop in the Regiment, we were going to have to "bring down" each of our Calvary vehicles for at least three weeks. This included all our tanks, scout vehicles, mortar tracks, armored personnel carriers, trucks and recovery vehicles.

After I shared the COLABORATION process I used to come to this conclusion, my CO finally agreed, and we received the orders to proceeded to dismantle all our vehicles.

As stated earlier, it was left to me, still a junior and relatively inexperienced Officer, to solve the first part of our problem: A way to get our troops to "CARE" about their vehicles and begin performing better first level maintenance in the desert fields.

I always believed that "ACTION" speaks louder than words, so I began personally checking engine oil and water levels of their vehicles both in the field and in the motor pool. With my new "hands on" actions happening, none of my troops wanted to be caught by me with low engine fluid levels or first level maintenance needs. If they did, they would receive the wrath of their Troop Executive Officer, yours truly! It was my way of showing that I cared about them and their equipment. They were all getting the message through my actions.

After all our equipment was repaired and back in top notch working order, we soon had our next two-week desert exercise approaching. Prior to our departure, I was called upon by my CO to give a speech to our entire Troop about the importance of us all keeping our equipment in good running order. Being only 22 years old, I was scared to death to give this talk. I had never spoken in front of 200+ people before, especially ones who had a lot more military experience than I.

With a deep breath, and believing in what I was about to share, I told our troops that our mission was to return from our two-week desert exercise with all vehicles running and to cross our final line of return with all weapons and equipment in good working order.

I shared with our troops to CARE for their vehicles and to treat them as if they were their own homes. We did not want to leave any of our troops, or their vehicles broken down or lost in the desert on this next mission. The room was very quiet as our men absorbed and understood what I was sharing.

For the first time in my life I realized I had delivered a speech which came from my heart and not my head. The power and truth from doing so was soon to follow which taught me a huge lesson: When possible, always gather your thoughts first, then speak from your heart with no notes or power points.

I was so proud when, after two weeks of grueling desert exercises, my all mobile Calvary Troop returned with 100% of our vehicles and weapons operational when we crossed the tactical return line. My Motor Sargent was crammed in the engine compartment of our last

Sheraton tank as it crossed the line. He was feverishly working on the engine to keep the tank moving as it "limped" over the line.

Talk about dedication and lessons learned. I will never forget my Motor Sargent's dedication and duty to help make our mission of 100% vehicles returning a realty and success. My jeep driver and I followed this last tank of our Unit in.

I will never forget the salute from our Regimental Commander and the "great job Lieutenant" he shouted out to me as we crossed the final return line. He was pre-notified via radio coms from our Squadron CO there was a good chance, after more than a year of training in the desert, we would be his first Troop to return with all their vehicles "running and 100% ready to fight."

This big first led the entire Regiment to follow our Troop's methods and processes to maintain their vehicles and train their troops for desert warfare. Talk about Sustainability and Scalability! A huge lesson learned to me from my RELATIONSHIPS, EXPERIENCES and EDUCATION in the military. Never be afraid to create disruption and try something new.

Chapter Seven

Ninety Percent of Life is Just Showing Up

As I learned later in life from my son Troy's Airforce recruiter, (in the military's view), our RELATIONSHIPS, (family, friends and co-workers), EXPERIENCES and EDUCATION are the three most important things in life. These three KEYS open our internal doors and allow us to grow and prosper. Think about your resume and what it expresses.

My military service, along with my education and new army relationships were all helping build my vision and awareness on how to experience a successful family and business life. On the wall just outside my MSI office, I have a plaque that reads "90% Of Life is Showing Up." The more experiences we have, the more fulfilling and successful our life will be.

My military service was the first big addition to my RELATIONSHIP, EXPERIENCE and EDUCATION buckets.

Another military leadership and lesson learned gifted me the often-quoted belief that "you can accomplish anything you set your mind to." Or, simply said, anything is possible if you have the willingness to do so.

My story begins after being up for two days straight on extended military desert "live tank fire" road marches. I was called to my CO's tent to receive our next day's mission. He said, Lieutenant, you will be leading the Troop tonight on our third straight extended desert night road march. We will be departing at 2200.

I looked at him and said, "but sir, my Troop has been patrolling the deserts for two straight nights and we are low on fuel, water, food and my men badly need sleep." My Commander looked at me and said, "Lieutenant, you have your marching orders." I saluted him and said, "yes sir".

I was then off down a dusty road in my jeep to share the marching orders with my tired, hungry and "needing more gas" team. All that night, while leading our Regiment with over 600 fighting vehicles, I had a great fear I would make a wrong turn and get the whole 600 vehicle, 5000-man Calvary Regiment lost.

We were under complete blackout conditions with no moon. Each vehicle followed one in front of the other by only two or three feet. Much to my relief, I followed my map correctly, made all the right turns, and delivered the Regiment safely to our objective just as the sun was peaking over the desert mountains. From that point on I was a firm believer in "all things are possible when we set our mind to it."

While Army life was busy, and when I was not on desert exercises, we for the most part had our weekends off. An army friend introduced Barbara and I to Angel Fire, New Mexico, where a new ski resort was being developed. We were flown to the resort with four other couples along with a lead salesperson from Baca Grande Corp, a company based in El Paso that was developing the resort.

After an inclusive all-expense paid weekend skiing at the resort, we were convinced by our salesperson to go visit and choose a lot to buy. Which, much to my surprise, we did.

This was my first "capital investment" which had a great Return on Investment (ROI) in many ways. This first ROI portion turned into the Baca Grande offering me a position as part time lead hunter. I would search and qualify other military buddies and invite them to an all-expense paid weekend flying to and skiing the weekend at Angel Fire. Sunday afternoon, I would join the team and we would search for a lot for each of my four couples.

It was an amazing job, as I got to ski and have fun, while learning how to sell real estate. I learned to "sell the dream" as the roads were not even yet built to the lots we sold. In addition, only a small part of the village in the Resort was completed along with the first stage of the ski area. All lots, roads and future development were displayed on huge maps of the area.

I became one of Baca Grande's top lead generators and helped close millions of dollars in resort real estate sales. I learned, from my training at Baca Grande (EDUCATION) and practical EXPERIENCES that I loved to sell. Today, I still have that very special plaque presented to me at a company meeting. Here I was in the Army and still finding time to sell. The over achiever Rick was beginning to grow and polish his leadership and selling skills.

Chapter Eight

Gaining Business Experience

Having earned five years leadership experience in the military, and the year being 1975, it was personally time for me to move on. Following my service to our country, I also felt a strong desire to follow in my father's footsteps as a business entrepreneur. (After losing his job at Holland Furnace, he went on to purchase a paint store which he turned into a very successful chain of paint stores throughout Western Michigan).

With my Business and Finance degree in pocket, I was ready to take on the business world. However, before following my passion to start a company, I knew I needed some experience working my college degrees in the real business world.

With that AWARENESS, I joined Hyatt Regency Hotels as a management trainee earning a whopping $600 a month. After applying and proving my leadership skills (EXPERIENCES) which I learned in the Army, I soon won a manager's position on the opening team of a brand new 711 room Hyatt Hotel being built in Phoenix, Arizona.

The hotel business at Hyatt Hotels was at first fun and exciting. After opening the hotel, I was soon promoted to Manager of the revolving rooftop restaurant: The Compass. The Compass, sitting on top of this beautiful new 711 room Hyatt Hotel, was soon drawing huge crowds.

One of many things I learned while managing the Compass team was the importance of listening to my employees and building trust and respect between all co-workers. The hostess', waiters, waitresses, bus boys and cooks were all proven professionals with big egos, and a desire to make a lot of money in tips. Getting them to all work together as a team was as big a challenge to me as it was in the military.

I was next promoted to Director of Catering and Convention services and was responsible for all the conventions and meetings held at the hotel. This required me to manage a team of over 1000 employees as we planned for, organized, and created the events. This included planning the meetings and catering meals for over 1500 guests at a time. A big lesson taught to me during this time was the importance of constant and consistent COMMUNICATION.

While gaining experience for Hyatt, my Chief and I once agreed to serve over 3000 Best Western conference attendees for dinner at our hotel with only six hours' notice. The event was originally to be held outside on the grounds of the Biltmore Hotel. However, it was pouring rain that day and all the Hyatt team at my hotel took on the challenge with much success.

Another EXPERIENCE where I learned that anything is possible when you set your mind to it! My "over achiever" self was kicking in big time.

As for me, the leader of the hotel team, I had a personal mission to "keep all employees and guests happy all the time." This personal mission demanded I be "on call" 24 hours a day while working at the hotel 12 to 15 hours, six days a week. In my view, it was always required for me to give first class service to my guests and my employees.

Back on the personal life, my wife Barbara had grown very tired of our constant moving and me being out in the desert or at work at the hotel as it seemed to her "24 hours a day seven days a week". One day, Barbara looked at me and asked me... "who are you?" This was the beginning of and soon led to my first divorce.

The big problem was the same we had when I was serving in the military: the lack of family time together. Our first five years I was always gone from home fighting in the desert, and our next four years I spent all my time in Hyatt ballrooms taking care of employees and guests. I had let my striving for success suck away most of my family time. I will never forget my feelings of shock when the divorce papers were served.

On top of that, my father passed away during the same miserable time I was going through my divorce. I was feeling hopeless, lonely, depressed and sad throughout the next seemingly never-ending months. It was all I could do to "put on my happy face" and be positive to my team when I showed up for work at the Hyatt. The second "BIG" mistake in my life which I learned so much from: steeling time from my loved ones and spending it at work.

This awful experience "woke me up" and gave me AWARENESS that I was "out of balance." It then took some time before I had complete ACCEPTANCE, of the fact I must seek change in my personal and future family life if I was to be so blessed. ACTION, ALLOWANCE and a good ATTITUDE were next needed to follow my dream and passion to start my own company, be married again, and start a family.

These "FIVE A's" became my street signs down a new road seeking a balanced, happy family and work life. As the Army taught me, situational AWARENESS, was a KEY.

That being learned, and with these new good and bad EXPERIENCES, I later made the decision to turn down an offer from Hyatt to run a new 1100 room hotel in Dallas, Texas. While giving the Hyatt two months' time as I turned over my many responsibilities, and for the next six months thereafter, I worked on my "first ever" Business Plans and my new life goals.

This led to the creation (in writing and on many Excel spreadsheets), my first company, Meeting Systems, Inc. (MSI 1)

Chapter Nine

Entrepreneur Keys which Start your Business

Meeting Systems, Inc. (MSI 1's) mission was to focus on "planning, coordinating, and operating conventions for corporate customers." With a personal check for $5,000, I went to the bank and opened my first MSI account. Little did I know, or even dream, this $5k MSI "startup" cash account would generate over $100m in cash flow over my next 40 years in business.

This was accomplished through a KEY MSI Guiding Principle that we followed in all three of my MSI startups: In our work priorities, our people (family and MSI team) are #1, our customers are #2 and all other matters follow as #3. This was the beginning of finding my KEYS to a positive and happy work / family / life balance.

As I also learned through my business experiences, a good business plan with annual Company Goals are KEYS to success. These PLANS lay the road map for a company to generate reoccurring revenue, to be scalable (the ability to grow in people, revenue and profits), be sustainable (forever or until sold) and to create a set of Guiding Principles with good values. These are KEYS to success in balancing your family and business life and which help you create excellent family and corporate cultures.

As leaders, we must establish these KEYS, and follow them with heart and soul. They are the positive path to creating a healthy and happy family along with a good company culture. At the end of the day, as a leader, it is a positive company culture you must create which will be the heart and engine driving your company.

The ability for you as a leader to DELEGATE with trust is a must if you wish to balance business and family life. Your ability to delegate will guide your team to be AWARE, ACCEPT and take ACTION when decisions must be made in your absence, be accountable for their actions, and always approach the implementation of their decisions with a good ATTITUDE.

Why is this important? It is the KEY for you building trust and respect for your leadership team and for them to build trust and respect for their employees. Trust and respect are a crucial to building solid and positive RELATIONSHIPS...one of our three most important things in life.

And why does this matter? I learned (and I hope you do too) that through delegation and trust of my team, I could go home early, coach my kids on the soccer fields, and spend quality time being emotionally and physically PRESENT for my wife and family in the evenings and weekends.

Only during rare people or customer emergencies, and when preparing our annual plans / budgets, would you find me working at home. I learned we could take extended family trips and the calls for help and or advice from my team were few and far between.

When I was away, my senior team always strived to make good decisions based on our guiding principles and business plans. Occasionally mistakes and wrong decisions were made. However, we all learned from these mistakes and grew as a team without my input and or hovering over them. DELEGATION allowed me to have fun with my family while my senior team was learning and running MSI without me being present. How did I get to this great family / business / life balance?

I guess you could say it first started with basic lessons I learned from building and running MSI 1. There, through a few good employees and good partnerships we created some positive cash flow as we followed our business plans. We successfully created and operated some major events and conferences at Meeting Systems Inc.

I learned that taking good care of and LISTENING to my people, customers and partners was another KEY balance in life. My customers and employees knew more about what was needed and going on in the field and ballrooms than I did. These EXPERIENCES were more "lessons for me."

Chapter Ten

The Power of Relationships

In 1985, After three good years of building and running MSI 1, I found it time to begin thinking about and creating a second business. My true passion was to start another new company that focused on creating technology for the automation of hotel sales and catering departments in large hotels.

Again, my serial Entrepreneur spirit was calling. I saw a great need for these software applications while working for Hyatt Hotels and my EDUCATION and EXPERIENCES were now motivating and guiding me to ACTION. I sold MSI1 to my partners and begin creating Multi-Systems, Inc. (MSI 2).

Unfortunately, I soon realized I knew absolutely nothing about technology, computers or software. And, worse yet, I had no RELATIONSHIPS in the computer or software industry. However, you will learn as I did, that there is no roadblock tough enough to stop an entrepreneur.

As I learned from my experiences in the Military, "anything is possible you set your mind and heart to." That being realized, I started searching for someone who understood computers and how-to develop software applications.

It was my good friend and hairdresser Jenny, (life's about RELATIONSHIPS) who introduced me to John Glitsos. John was a salesman for Prime Computers and claimed he also knew "a little about" how to write software programs. He liked my ideas on creating Hotel applications and the size of the potential market. So, we teamed up, and went searching for seed money to fund my second new startup, Multi-Systems, Inc.

John's old boss at Prime funded us $20k, and a friend and Hyatt customer of mine agreed to fund another $20k. That cost me 10% of the company to John, 10% to each of our "friend and family" investors and left me owning 70% of MSI 2. Not bad I thought at the time. My RELATIONSHIPS were paying off!

Speaking about RELATIONSHIPS, and back on a personal note, it was about this time I met my second wife Joni. We met at a mutual friends Thanksgiving party and soon found ourselves dating. One year later we were married. Four years later, I was blessed to have three wonderful sons; twins Troy, & Cody and two years later came Luke. They soon became the "loves of my life" and were true treasures and teachers to me.

I learned from my three sons' that the greatest gift in life is our children. And we can learn more from our children than anywhere, anyplace or anything in our lives. My three sons have taught me so much (EDUCATION), led me to more EXPERIENCES and brought more RELATIONSHIPS into my life than I ever could have dreamed of. My trust and respect for them will be forever honored and treasured.

Back to MSI 2, we were soon buying computers and developing software. For the next four years, I found myself happily growing and running my second technology company. During those years, we raised over $400K in bank financing and $1M in Venture capital funding. Unfortunately, I soon found the venture capitalist were "in control" of MSI. After two rounds of funding, they soon owned over 50% of MSI 2 stock and my ownership percent dwindled to only 15%.

I must admit all my attorneys warned me that "taking the cash and losing control" and "majority stake" of your company was a very slippery slope and a dangerous road to travel. As my attorneys also warned, The VC's now had control of "my" company and most of MSI.

Only one year later, MSI was in a tailspin and running out of cash. We desperately needed our planned and "VC promised" third round of financing as our cash flow projections indicated.

Undenounced to me, MSI's lead venture capitalist, Gray Hound Capital, (who had a seat on MSI's Board), had locked up all their venture funding when they moved their offices from Phoenix to the East Coast. SunVen Partners, (our second group of VCs') also had an MSI board seat.

Unfortunately, about this same time, their MSI Board member developed cancer and was forced to resign his Board seat. This caused SunVen to also freeze any additional MSI VC funding. All of this was happening right at the point where MSI's business plan called for the third round of VC financing.

MSI was running out of cash fast. So, I worked with our attorneys and created a proposed "reverse buy out" from my VC partners at our next Board Meeting.

This Plan created a way for me to buy the VC stock back through additional "family and friends" cash and a with a very low MSI evaluation. The Plan freed the VC's to "write off their MSI losses" and walk away from MSI with no contingent liabilities. I was very nervous (scared to death was more like it), when we called the MSI Board meeting where my plan for the VC reverse stock buyback was to be presented.

After a two-hour intense meeting, and much to my shock, the Board voted against my plan. They voted instead to declare Chapter 7 bankruptcy and immediately close the company. This, even though

MSI was soon to begin turning a profit. The VC's were concerned about customers and or employees "breaching the Corporate Shell."

This occurrence would possibly make the existing Board members personally liable if MSI were to be sued for failure to deliver on existing Agreements. A sorry argument and a Board decision based on fear as far as I was concerned. At that moment, I was mad, and felt very much let down by my VC partners.

A day after my last MSI 2 Board meeting, I had feelings of utter devastation. A few days later (as I learned later from my friends) I fell into mourning for the loss of my company. MSI 2 was soon in total "shut down" Chapter 7 bankruptcy.

I had to permanently close MSI's doors, and send 65 dedicated employees' home with no work, no pay, and customers left unsupported. Me included!

I now knew exactly how my father felt many years ago when he too was sent home and out of work due to his company being shut down.

After this EXPERIENCE and licking my wounds by creating a personal journal of my mistakes and lesson learned EXPERIENCES, I began working with a Judge and my attorneys to sell all MSI 2 assets.

This led me to a humbling conclusion; "Life is a daring adventure, or nothing at all" as originally quoted by Hellen Keller. This all took place in four short years from 1980 to 1985.

Chapter Eleven

Life's Daring Adventure as a Risk Taker

After a lot of tears, self-introspect, and creating my journal about "what went wrong," I picked myself up and was hired by IPCS as Vice President of Sales and Marketing. IPCS focused on creating and supporting software and systems technology for hotels. I was back in my element and re-discovering the POWER of a POSITVE ATTITUDE.

After four years (1986 to1990) at IPCS as Vice President of Sales and Marketing, through these years, I EXPERIENCED much more about leading company teams and developing and selling technology for the hospitality industry.

However, in December 1989, I was dismayed (and shocked) to discover that IPCS was being sold to Hospitality Franchise Systems, (HFS). Worse, HFS was going to close the technology group in Phoenix and turn the work over to EDS in Dallas, Texas. This would soon put me and 100 other employees out of work. Oh boy! Out of work, no job, and no paycheck again.

This circumstance was becoming very trying and demanding on me. However, "where there is a daunting challenge, one can find a new opportunity." As it turned out, IPCS needed me to remain and help with all the customer and product transitions to HFS and EDS.

I felt needed again and enjoyed what I learned and EXPERIENCED working for a large corporate entity.

After six months of working for HFS and still, after all I experienced, being a "serial entrepreneur" I took another big risk. My belief that "life is a daring adventure" was still alive and well!

After much thought and many business plans, I approached HFS and offered to purchase the technology and licensing rights to the hotel industry software they would no longer going to provide to hotels outside of the HFS hotel group.

I also very much wanted to begin supporting the existing customer base that were not HFS hotels and which were generating reoccurring revenue. Of course, I did not have the $400K HFS soon decided all these software assets and customers were worth. So, I proposed a creative deal. I offered HFS a 10% commission on all the software I sold for the next five years up to maximum of $500k.

After many weeks of intense negotiations and contract drafts we closed the deal. Wow, another new and exciting entrepreneur adventure was starting to become a reality for me!

During our negotiations, I had the opportunity to create a new company and corporate structure to support the deal. So, in 1990, much to my excitement and delight, I founded MSI 3 as a "Phoenix Arisen" Multi-Systems, Inc. For my third time, I had new opportunities, new risks, and a firm Contract with a publicly traded company (HFS) to "produce and deliver" per the terms of our Agreement. If I failed to deliver, I was certain I would find myself back at my attorney's office begging and paying big sums of money for their help and support.

Over the next 30 years, we grew MSI 3 from one employee (myself) to over 200 employees. After a few years, together as a solid MSI team following our Guiding Principles and annual business plans, we soon were producing over $20 million in consistent new annual sales and reoccurring revenue from our 6000-hotel customer base. I did learn from my EXPERIENCE of losing my second MSI to venture capitalist and bank loans to never find myself on this path again.

During the new MSI 3 growing times, I thought a lot about my father, and what I learned from him, when he came home fired from his company, job and career. And how I felt, after having the same happen to me after we had to close the doors at MSI 2.

That being said - and learned, I grew my third and "greatest" MSI 3 with no "friends and family" financing, no debt and no Venture Capital.

Instead, I was now smart enough to focus on positive cash flow from customers and their reoccurring maintenance revenue. This was all produced by a first-class Customer Support Department, second to none Sales, Marketing and Finance Teams, and the Hospitality Industry's best Product Management, Software Engineering, and Quality Assurance teams.

These MSI teams worked seamlessly together through great COMMUNICATION to provide the very best integrated hardware and software solutions for our Hospitality Industry customers.

Chapter Twelve

Growing the Business

As we grew, we created with the help of our attorneys, a very successful MSI Incentive Stock Option (ISO) program which encouraged my employees to "own a part" of the company. There is nothing like owning a piece of the company you work for to help motivate you to work smart and make the right decisions.

Over the next 18 years, that program ended up with employees owning 20% of the company. I highly recommend ISO programs if you wish to share your equity with senior employees. I loved it when I heard my employees referring to MSI as "my company." I did retain ownership of the remaining 80% of the company over the next 18 years.

In additions, we made two major company purchases in the first 10 years of being in business. One was from Pegasus for the purchase of all the licensing and sales rights to their Nova Plus hotel property management system. This was a very sweet deal as we agreed to take on support for their 600 installed hotels. Of course, along with the deal, MS was to receive all the recurring monthly maintenance revenue generated from Nova Plus properties. MSI purchased all assets along with the software licensing and support agreements. We also agreed to hire all the Pegasus' employees required to support the Nova Plus products and hotels. The deal was mutually rewarding. MSI paid no cash at all to Pegasus. Instead, we agree to develop a two-way interface to the Best Western Central reservation system and pay all expenses related to the project. MSI also agreed to take on all liabilities for the outstanding contracts Pegasus had to their existing Nova Plus customer base. In the exchange, Pegasus received a big tax right off from losses they incurred from their original purchase of Nova Plus. This made the deal a "win-win."

For further understanding of the deal, The Nova Plus interface to the Best Western CRS was promised by Pegasus to Nova Plus properties at their time of the Nova Plus purchase. However, after four years of trying to build this technology, the interface had still not been delivered.

Pegasus' failure to deliver the CRS interface had created lawsuits from their properties and from Best Western corporate. However, as stated earlier, the purchase of Nova Plus by MSI was consummated only after MSI agreed to take on all the liability and responsibility to build the two way Best Western interface.

Gulp!! If we were not ORGANIZED and delivered as promised, I took the risk of being back at our attorney's office with another MSI biting the dust.

Much to my relief, after only six months of dedicated focus, my MSI team had completed the CRS interface. It took AWARENESS, ACCEPTANCE, ACTION, ALLOWANCE and a good ATTITUDE to 'make it happen". As my father had taught me and I kept repeating to the team, lets "DO IT RIGHT" the first time.

Our second purchase was RemCO a company based in Dickinson, South Dakota. The transaction included all assets, including licensing rights and monthly support agreements for their existing 2000 installed hotels. This transaction was completed through a $2M cash purchase and a four-year MSI 'stock earn of' 10% of MSI outstanding shares of stock.

The purchase and integration with MSI of the South Dakota based RemCO team and their international customers was a complete success. A big challenge for me personally was integrating the more than 100 RemCO employees with the MSI team from their remote location in North Dakota. It took much patience, good COMMUNICATION and many trips for "face to face" meetings.

Integrating two corporate cultures is always a challenge. Fortunately, Remco had a similar culture as MSI. They took good care of their employees and customers which is was one of the main reasons we made the purchase in the first place. Again, for the MSI team, it was necessary to use the MSI Five A's as we plowed through the purchase and integration of RemCO with the MSI team.

AWARNESS, ACCEPTANCE, ACTION, ALLOWANCE and a good ATITUDE was the name of the game.

I am driven to thank David Berkus, of Berkus LLC, MSI's truly professional outside Consultant and my personal mentor. David guided us through the purchase and integration of RemCO. When you find a good consultant, you can personally TRUST and RESPECT, they become invaluable to you as CEO and the success of your company.

I encourage you to find a Mentor / Consultant and depend on him / her for help as you grow your business and find yourself with perplexing problems which must be solved. Again, Gulp! MSI took on a big responsibly with tremendous risk of losing customers and employees after the transaction. My fear did not happen, and for this, I am forever grateful. As an entrepreneur, we must be willing to take risk, ask for help, listen (to our employees, customers and consultants) and finally, take action and cause disruption when called for.

Chapter Thirteen

The Balance of Business and Family

Unfortunately, though all this, I lost focus on my wife Joni, while being laser focused on my three sons and MSI 3. The day after we got home from a Mediterranean Cruise in 2008, I went to the office and opened my briefcase. In it was a two-page letter from Joni which included the fact she was, "as I read this letter" moving out of our home. She was "only moving a few miles" away and trusted the fact that I would take good care of the boys while she filed for divorce.

I felt devasted as there was no talk or pre-warning of Joni's decision to move out. On top of that, as stated earlier, we had just returned from a two-week vacation cruise in Europe. Talk about family disruption!

My only choice was to "keep moving forward" and doing what I knew I was good at and learned so far: raising sons and growing a business. After phone calls and many meetings with my close friends, my lesson learned was we can't control People, Places and Things.

All we can truly do is control how we react to the circumstances, be positive, and "live in the moment." Joni had made the decision to divorce me, and there was no "changing of minds" or gong back. My life had to move on and my Five A's kicked in. The hardest "A" to get through at the time was the second: ACCEPTANCE. It was a new and very difficult road in life for all of us. However, after a tough two years, Joni, Troy, Cody, Luke and I came to a very positive intersection on that road, made a RIGHT, and all were again happy.

How did we accomplish our business successes and still get through these family and life experiences? We stuck to our personal values and Guiding Principles.

I say "we" because it was important to me all MSI managers and associates knew my family was my primary focus and my next priority was taking care of them...all my Associates. To ensure all associates were on the same page, the MSI Team worked together to create and publish a new revision of our Guiding Principles and Values. Our Guiding Principles were reviewed with the team and updated annually. Each employee was requested to keep a hard copy posted in plain sight on their desk. (See a complete version of MSI Guiding Principles at the end of The Appendix).

Our Guiding Principles with values had their beginnings when I put together many of the lessons learned from my EDUCATION and EXPERIENCES generated during my years in the Army and at HYATT. At MSI 2, I also began sending at least one email a day thanking an employee for a specific customer or team accomplishment which I heard about from a manager or read about in an email.

We also featured a monthly Spinnaker award which were a documented "thank you" given for individual "actions and results" which helped either a customer or a fellow associate. The proposed awards were submitted directly to me by any associate in the company. After my approval it was accepted and included in a monthly Spinnaker award document sent to all employees. By doing so, each employee was able to see how a fellow associate helped a customer or fellow associate improve service or solve a problem.

(For those of you who are not sailors a Spinnaker is the LEADING sail on a sailboat when sailing down wind.)

These awards helped all employees strive to improve their work, creativity and decisions so they too would receive a Spinnaker award and the resulting total company recognition.

At the end of the year in December, the MSI Senior Team reviewed and added up all the Spinnaker awards given out for the year and then chose a "Spinnaker of the Year" associate. That employee received a $4000 check at our MSI annual meeting...and a lot of recognition in front of all MSI associates.

AT MSI 3, in addition to the above at MSI 2, we also recognized an employee of the Quarter and employee of the Year whom were also chosen by the MSI senior team. An email was sent out each Quarter announcing the winner and why they were chosen.

In addition, an MSI plaque was custom made for each of these associates to place in his or her office. We also placed a gold band with their name and the Quarter on large annual Master Plaques placed on an" Honors Wall" outside our MSI employee cafeteria. At our annual meeting, the associate of the year was announced with much fanfare by me, the CEO.

Chapter Fourteen

The Business Planning Process

In addition, MSI had a Five-year Plan along with very well documented, organized, and collaborated Corporate Goals, Departmental Goals, Annual Budgets (based on our goals) and Employee Reviews. Firm delivery timelines for each of the above deliverables were reviewed and agreed upon by the management team.

Starting in September, the MSI Senior team would work hard to hash out all agree upon a very well-defined set of 10 to 12 MSI Corporate Goals for the next year. Next, the Senior and Finance Teams would hammer out the annual Budgets needed to support these goals including a capital expenditure list, revenue and expense projections.

These projections included a well-documented attachment of the new employees along with job descriptions needed to support the Corporate Goals and Annual Budget.

At the beginning of October, the Corporate Goals and Annual Projections were submitted to the entire management team for their review, collaboration and ACCEPTANCE. Once all managers completely understood and agreed on the Corporate Goals and Projections, each Department Head was required to create and submit to the Senior Team their departmental goals and projections which supported MSI Corporate Goals. All goals had a required completion date the end of November.

Finally, to complete the annual MSI planning process, employee reviews were given to each employee by their manager during December. (See our employee review form at the end of The Appendix).

MSI Employee reviews followed well documented MSI guidelines for performance and personal values consistency. In addition, each employee review required five to six individual action goals which supported their departmental goals along with one or two personal goals. All Employee reviews were required to be completed and turned in to our Personnel Department by the end of the calendar year.

Chapter Fifteen

Goals, Budgets and Reviews

It amazed me how effective MSI's three-month "Goal, Budgets, and Reviews' planning process helped with the leadership, delegation and assistance for our managers "to make the right choices" throughout the year.

The planning process required good communication and insured the entire MSI team was rowing at the same beat in the same direction. After a few years of perfecting the process, MSI's Annual Budget (which had grown to over $20m) was consistently within a few thousand dollars of meeting our annual revenue and expense projections. On the Corporate and Departmental Goal side, we were soon meeting an average of 80% of our goals.

In addition to the above, MSI conducted annual Gallup Surveys for all employees....me included. (See our Gallup Survey form at the end of the Appendix). The Gallup Surveys, once completed by the end of September, were tallied up by each department and shared with the MSI Senior Team. It was amazing to me how effective the surveys were in pointing out faults and needs within each department. Talk about a good way to implement change!

After reading and researching recaps of each departmental Gallup review, department heads submitted to the Management team the people changes needed and additional equipment and other resources needed to address the findings in our Gallop Surveys. I highly recommend these surveys as a wonderful way to LISTEN to your employees and make positive change that will be noticed by your entire Team. The surveys only cost 10 minutes with each employee. The Return on Investment (ROI) was very positive.

Finally, I cannot stress enough the importance of having a well thought out, Senior Team approved, and all employee published company Organization Chart. Your Org chart must be very clear, and the lines of authority focused on "who reports to whom" within your company. I reviewed MSI's Org Chart every six months and was amazed at how quickly the "informal Org Chart" takes over and replaces the published Org Chart.

In some cases, the informal reporting line changes are good...and other times they can be very bad as employees grab on to "power positions" to force their authority. When your "AWARENESS" of these changes kicks in its time to visit with your department heads to see if a change or "ACTION" is required. You can then determine if change is required to the formal Org chart or if certain employees or managers need to be reminded of the existing Org chart's lines of authority.

I found the best way to discover these "informal changes" as they crop up are to occasionally walk around your company and ask select employees what they are working on and who's helping. Your employees will be excited to know you care what they are focused on and will be more than happy to share their projects and any concerns or roadblocks.

To ensure each manager and employee knows what their authority and responsibilities are within your organization it is also critical that well defined and employee shared Position Descriptions are created and agreed upon. Once your Position Descriptions are created, it is important that you review them with your employees during their annual review. This is the time they can be refreshed to ensure that what your managers and employees are focused on meets the requirements in their Position Descriptions. (See a sample of MSI's Position Description at the end of the Appendix).

Chapter Sixteen

Reflections for your success

Perhaps this chapter's contents may be my most important contribution to your success. Here are seven concepts I created or learned and then internalized over the years to balance personal and business life, and to honor family as well as associates. I'll include the detail of these, such as the first, "Guiding Principles," and the second, "The Five A's" after each, so that you might adopt those that strike you as important for your life's balance. Here they are…

1. Follow your Guiding Principles

The power of praise and positive recognition for both teamwork and individuals at meetings and "one on ones" was learned and practiced by me during my Army and Hyatt leadership days. After starting my first MSI, I soon discovered myself following these Educated and Experienced "praising and thank you" ways as I founded and grew MSI 2 and MSI 3. I found myself feeling positive inside when handing out individual thank you's for both good teamwork and individual successful actions for fellow employees and our customers. These feelings were present when I took these ACTIONS both one and one and our meetings. What was important was that I remained authentic while expressing my gratitude.

Back on a personal note, a few years after founding MSI 3, I was very blessed to meet and work with my third wife Connie, who was an associate on our MSI sales and marketing team. Over the next four years we traveled together with the MSI team and became close associates as we took care of our employees and customers. Connie eventually left MSI to focus on raising her family. During this time, I also served on the Board of Directors of the Phoenix Crisis Nursery. We worked with AZ Child Protective Services and helped and housed children who were abused by their parents. The Crisis Nursery soon became in need of a Marketing Manager for promoting our cause to "break the cycle of child abuse". I thought Connie may be the ideal person for this position as I knew she loved children. We became "reconnected" after I reached out to Connie to see if she would be interested in the opportunity at the Crisis Nursery. Connie was unfortunately un-able to take that position due to travel distance to the Nursery from her home.

However, a few short months later, Connie agreed to begin working part time at MSI and soon became MSI's full time Marketing Manager. When Connie rejoined MSI, we were going through troubled times with major difficulties converting our customers from MSI's Windows based Property Management System to our new Cloud based PMS. Connie reminded me of the importance of our Guiding Principles when she wrote a very powerful Press Release on how MSI was following our Guiding Principle when we provided a new CloudPM system and exceptional service for an existing customer. This customer had given us a very positive case study using the MSI new CloudPM property management system.

I will be forever grateful how Connie helped me and the MSI team focus and get back on our path of following MSI's Guiding Principles. Our focused efforts lead MSI out of the rough patch and back onto the positive revenue growth path. Flash forward five years later and we were happily married in March 2013. Connie joined me with five wonderful children of her own. We are now very blessed to have a blended family of ten. I have found my forever soul mate and the most important RELATIONSHIP in my life.

So, here come MSI's Guiding Principles.

MSI Guiding Principles

We are unified in our purpose to be of service to our associates and customers as we exceed expectations.

We deliver the technology and services we promise and respect our business partnerships.

We continually improve and enhance our products and services.

We openly communicate, have trustworthy relationships and honor all opinions.

We work as a team and respect each other. Our doors are always open for discussion.

We seek to understand the facts, make informed decisions, and are unified in support of those decisions.

Positive, corrective action takes precedence over assigning blame.

We are committed to integrity in all that we say and do.

We lead and serve by example.

We foster ongoing personal and professional development for all associates.

We set goals, define objectives, establish budgets and are profitable.

We seek humility, honor and gratitude in all our endeavors.

We are about having fun!

2. The Five "A's"

In 2016 I successfully and profitably sold MSI to a Canadian publicly traded company, Jonas Software, Inc. I have stayed on as a consultant and MSI continues to grow and be profitable under the leadership and added capital resources of Jonas. I soon began helping other entrepreneurs in Phoenix learn how to grow their companies with reoccurring revenue and teaching the importance of being "scalable and profitable." I also found myself, with much happiness and pleasure, being a business advisor to Arizona State University business students wishing to start their own companies and "learn some lessons" from the EXPERIENCES of a serial entrepreneur, yours truly.

As stated earlier, I will never forget one of my students' questions: "Rick, how in the world did you find the time to successfully take care of and grow a family, while, at the same time, successfully taking care of and growing a business?" How did you "discover this magic time balance?" This question has been asked of me many times before and is the foundation and the spirit from which I created this book.

As also stated earlier, this book contains all my lessons learned on the power of building scalability and sustainability into your company while focusing on positivity and persistence while growing your business and loving your family and life. The power of my FIVE A's philosophy in managing family, business and life balance gave me strategic, tactical and spiritual guidance. AWARENESS, ACCEPTANCE, ACTION, ALLOWANCE AND ATTITUDE were the keys. The following is my FIVE "A'S DOCUMENT:

"The Five A's"

As I reflect on 2015, I feel "mission accomplished" as we completed our 25th year of business at MSI. Over the years, as we evolved into a cloud property management solutions company for the hospitality industry, I think about how MSI arrived here. No doubt our success, and that of each team member, is directly related to adhering to MSI Guiding Principles and properly managing our lives.

Each of us has numerous opportunities for growth, whether personally or professionally. Recognizing this is, in part, key to success. Another factor is in understanding our role in the endeavor and accepting the responsibility we have before us. However, if we sit idly by, even with our thinking caps on, we hinder our progress; we must be do-er's. Not everything will go the way we plan; life is a fast-changing world. So, we learn to adapt and course-correct. It must be that simple, right? Perhaps it's all a matter of attitude.

The following is what I like to call "The Five A's." For years I've found these to be beneficial in helping others to make informed decisions, find success by implementing its simple philosophy, and hopefully live more happily. I share them with you here.

Awareness

"80 percent of success is just showing up" — *Woody Allen*

To be fair, the quote outside my office door says its 90 percent, but who's counting? I believe we can compromise at 85 percent and suffice to say it's a pretty big number either way. Showing up means awaking to a new day and new possibilities—it's possibly the most important work. It's being aware.

When we "show up," we are saying we are aware of situations, regardless of our feelings about them. We are seeing and experiencing for ourselves versus being told so by someone else or viewing in written word. While we may not be present at every juncture, we know we are doing our part when we show up and deliver on our commitments. As a Veteran, I refer to this as the military does: "situational awareness."

Acceptance

"Experience is what you get when you didn't get what you wanted."
— Italian proverb

Once we have awareness, accepting the outcome of a situation "is what it is" can be empowering. We may not get the results we expected, but when we have put forth our best, we will come away with more experience. This will ultimately help us in the future if we accept it and learn from it. We can always try to accept the things we cannot change. There is no benefit to fighting the outcome, being angry or fearful about it. We cannot change people, places, and things. Acceptance is key.

Action

"Deliberation is the work of many men. Action, of one alone." —
Charles de Gaulle

Being aware of and accepting of a situation is only half the battle. We must now take action. The move we make may be because we don't like where we are in life or wish to alter the course of our efforts in an undertaking. Sometimes simply showing up can help move us toward our goal. It takes courage to change the things we can. On rare occasions, taking action may also mean you need do nothing ... which is a form of action.

Allowance

In baiting a mouse trap with cheese, always leave room for the
mouse." — Saki [Hector Hugh Monro]

We can overdo some things and wind up not having room for what's most desired. When we think about opening to allowance, it's as if we open a gate and make room for situations to happen naturally—without coercion or traps. This is risky, you say? It can also be empowering. Try exercising a little faith and a glimmer of hope. The situation will play out, once any course corrections are made. In due time the end will be revealed. Avoid over-thinking, over-promising, and under-delivering. These *will* inevitably trap us. Know all things happen for a reason and as they should.

Attitude

"We may affirm absolutely that nothing great in the world has been accomplished without passion." — *Georg Wilhelm Friedrich Hegel*

If you can align your attitude about your work, you may develop a passion for success in that which you do. The power we exert in our attitude about any situation has the ability to transform us—possibly even the situation itself and those involved in it. Be assured it can alter your perception in any challenge you face. We can all strive to be positive, kind, and helpful as we travel through life. Our attitudes speak loudly that great things can and will happen. Here's to success!

3. The Four Agreements in Business, Family and Life

Over the past 40 years, I have founded and grown three successful companies and have raised over $3 million in venture capital and bank funding. I have hired or acquired over 3000 associates during my entrepreneurial career and led over 2000 managers and employees. I also discovered a passion while creating all these experiences. My most valuable passion in running a business, and the gift I receive is my love for helping and supporting my associates as they grow professionally while helping their families grow with them.

Over these years, (and I'm grateful for all I've learned from my children), I discovered a passion and developed a love for coaching youth sports including soccer, basketball, baseball and flag football. I coached my three sons, along with their sports teams, from age 4 to 15, in all three sports year around. I have coached over 500 soccer, basketball, baseball, and flag football games for youth sports over these years. I was also a soccer youth sports team leader and organizer. In that role, I found myself putting the youth teams together and settling all the "coach, parent, child" requests, concerns and challenges. Boy, what I learned from the EXPERIENCES from all these conflicts and requests! I learned a lot about leadership, dispute resolution, and the power of good communication. All lessons I brought to work with me and applied, taught and shared with the MSI management team.

I was also very active in my sons schooling as they navigated the fun and challenges of grade school. I was President of the Kiva PTO (my boys' elementary school) and founder and President of the Kiva Dads Club. I am also past President and current Vice President of our Home Owners association and am very active in our community.

I have been a member and Sunday school teacher at three different churches over my 60 years including Protestant, Catholic, and

Mormon religions. Many wonderful, rich and spiritual EXPERIENCES and LESSONS have been delivered to me on my spiritual journeys. These include how to "live in the moment," being forever grateful and knowing there is a Higher Power than you.

I have also studied and taught the Mastery of Love during a focused three-year period.   And have been coaching and living this spiritual wisdom of love, faith and gratitude over the past 15 years. The main lesson learned from the Mastery: Always choose love over fear. Only love is real.... all else is an illusion. At the end of the day, we all want to feel needed and feel loved.

We all need something to do, someone to love, and something to hope for. Let go and let God. Surrender. Be vulnerable. Progress not Perfection. Move forward with faith service and love, leave the fear behind. This will always keep you on the High road of life. I truly believe it is these spiritual EXPERIENCES, EDUCATION and RELATIONSHIPS that have also been golden KEYS in guiding me and keeping me focused on a positive LIFE path.

In addition to coaching the MSI team and modeling the above values, I also conducted monthly classes at MSI for all new hires on the book, *The Four Agreements*. This was part of the MSI teams continuing EDUCATION program. Over the years, as a servant leadership coach for my many MSI employees and as a leader coaching youth sports, I've learned that the Four Agreements always apply.

The first Agreement is to be impeccable with your word. Always be in your integrity, say what you mean, do what you say, and always tell the truth. The second Agreement is to never assume.   To accomplish this, always insure you have good COMMUNICATION within your teams and throughout your company at all times. The third Agreement is to not take things personally. Know and believe that negative communication from a customer or an employee is not about you personally. The communication is about the situation, not you. The fourth Agreement is to always do your personal best. At the end of the day, this takes away all feelings of "I could of or should have done more". (See our Four Agreements pledge at the end of page 62).

As I have spoken earlier in this book, Trust and Respect are the major KEYS to good RELATIONSHIPS. These keys will help you be successful at growing your company while balancing a good family life. Respect is liking someone. Wanting to be connected to them. Respect is a positive energy you feel when you are around them. Wanting to communicate, be open, transparent and being vulnerable shows respect. When you respect, you learn to trust.

You trust the person you respect knowing they will be there for you, defend you, and most important honor and trust you. When you respect, you try not to judge, be angry, or resentful. To respect is to love, as fear is to resent and be jealous. When my neighbor buys a new car, I can choose to resent them (fear) because they have more than me, or I can choose to respect them, as they have earned the money to purchase the new car. I can honor and respect my brother when he earns an "A" in class, or I can resent and be jealous because he's "better than me".

Respect has unique levels and qualities based on the position and title of the person in your relationship. Respect for your spouse (partner), parents, sibling, friend, boss, teacher, coach, pet or drill sergeant all have varying levels, degrees, and characteristics of the love / respect you may have for them. When you respect your partner, you want to help them, be with them, do fun things with them, work with them, learn from them, grow with them and feel free to ask personal questions of them.

You want to be connected, love them, share your feelings, be affectionate, be vulnerable, learn and apply their Love Languages and trust them. When you respect your partner, you trust / love yourself. And when you trust / love yourself, you have no fear to share with your partner what behavior or actions are upsetting to you. Or share what you may not like about their actions in your relationship, or a character / behavior that is bothering or worrisome. Likewise, you have no fear, and try not to become defensive, when your partner shares upsetting behaviors with you. There is no fear in the relationship to have open honest communication about your faults.

We are human, and we all have our faults. However, we do want to stay focused on the positive side of the energy cycle and not the negative. We want to focus on expressing our gratitude for those behaviors and actions we are grateful for. When we focus on the good, the good gets better, and the faults diminish. Words of affirmation always trump criticism and complaining.

This is what I call the peanut butter sandwich approach to helping be authentic with our partner. The gratitude (yummy bread) on top then the "driving me nuts" (peanuts) inside, followed by another piece of the yummy bread. When you trust your partner, you will communicate your thoughts, feelings and fears with them, unconditionally. A good foundation of respect, trust and communication builds a positive energy relationship of unconditional love. It also helps us to stay in our truth and be authentic.

So, on the next page are the four agreements. Thanks to Don Michael Ruiz for these.

MSI FOUR AGREEMENTS
Don Miguel Ruiz

Be Impeccable with Your Word
Speak with integrity. Say only what you mean. Avoid using the word to speak against yourself or to gossip about others. Use the power of your word in the direction of truth and love.

Don't Take Anything Personally
Nothing others do is because of you. What others say and do is a projection of their own reality, their own dream. When you are immune to the opinions and actions of others, you won't be the victim of needless suffering.

Don't Make Assumptions
Find the courage to ask questions and to express what you really want. Communicate with others as clearly as you can to avoid misunderstandings, sadness, and drama. With just this one agreement, you can completely transform your life.

Always Do Your Personal Best
Your best is going to change from moment to moment; it will be different when you are healthy as opposed to sick. Under any circumstance, simply do your best and you will avoid self-judgment, self-abuse, and regret.

4. Servant Leadership

Back on my personal side, I love racing sailboats and was an award-winning Hobe cat racer. I've hiked the Grand Canyon and white water rafted on a seven-day camping adventure down the Colorado River with my twin sons Cody and Troy when they were only 10 years old. I have taken my three sons on a safari to Tanzania, Africa and seen the great animal migration. I have adventured with my family on many trips through Canada, Mexico and Europe, including a Mediterranean cruise to Venice, cruise to Alaska and a Baltic Seas cruise to Scandinavia and Russia.

We then went on to experience the many beauties of Ireland and Iceland. My three sons and I are expert snow skiers and we have skied throughout the USA together. We play spike ball on the beach and ski double black diamond runs through the trees. We love hiking and have climbed Camelback Mountain in under 30 minutes to the top. These experiences have allowed us all to learn, grow and thrive.

I love teaching, coaching and counseling friends, families and business leaders in servant leadership and living a life of love and gratitude. How can you be a servant leader? Listen to your people, then listen some more. Connect with your people. Watch and learn their body language. Be with them. Know their names. Ask them how they feel? Ask for their collaborative help in setting goals and objectives. Have empathy for them. Love them.

Use love and logic on them. Discipline with love, but firmness when necessary. Get to know their families. Help their families when you can. Physically touch your employees as appropriate and use eye contact whenever you can. Lesson Learned: Your leaders, associates and customers all know a lot more then you do... LISTEN TO THEM!

Servant Leadership and TIME: I taught Servant leadership at MSI using a clock analogy. There are four quadrants to a clock. The first quadrant being MSI people and how we must focus on both our families and our employees.

The second quadrant being MSI products and services that are scalable and generate reoccurring revenue. The third quadrant is MSI sales, marketing and customer service. In this quadrant, our focus is on generating new revenue while taking excellent care of our customers and exceeding their expectations. The fourth quadrant of our time at MSI was spent on financial planning, internal controls and being consistent.

This focus was on making sure we were following our strategic and tactical plans, tracking our budgets and monitoring our monthly financial statements to insure we were generating the budgeted and expected profits.

At home, on the garage door my family walks through every day, we have posted (on an actual ruler) the Golden Rule: Do unto others as you would have them do unto you. My three sons viewed this rule / value every day as they were growing up. In addition, I made sure I demonstrated this value anytime I could. I believe we cannot teach values; we can only demonstrate them to our children and our employees. This, I believe, is practicing good servant leadership.

5. Corporate Culture

My short summary story: When I graduated from college, which I paid for by working while in school, I had no money. I went into the army, got out of the Army, and had no money. I went to work for Hyatt and left five years later with $5000 in the bank. I next started my first MSI. I folded that company into a partner's travel company for no cash. I started my second MSI on an idea of creating hotel software applications. I knew nothing about computer programming or engineering to start this company. We grew, it lasted five years, and we went bankrupt.

I started my third MSI and grew it to a $20 million company. In college I only had a 2.7 grade point average. I grew my companies based on good corporate cultures, my sales & marketing skills and my willingness to be of service morning, day and night to take good care of our people and our customers.

Corporate Culture, and how to create a good one, is in the news a lot these days. In my view as a servant leader there is nothing more important for you as an entrepreneur than to start your company with the "end in mind" of creating and sustaining a good corporate culture. Good corporate culture is based on a well-thought-out set of guiding principles, good core values, and a mission statement that is clearly defined and communicated at Quarterly meetings. Likewise, when exiting your company, there is nothing more important than leaving with an excellent corporate culture. This will be your true legacy as a good leader. In your absence, your company will continue to thrive and grow.

At the end of the day, you will be asking to see your children and your family, not your company.

In summary, I believe our greatest teachers are our children and our employees. If you listen, watch and observe them many treasures will be gifted to you. The answer to the question can you run a company as an entrepreneur and still raise a successful family? I must first share I am so very grateful for all I have learned from my children. They have been the best teachers in my life. That being said the answer is yes. Being an entrepreneur and being blessed with a wonderful family are both possible together at the same time.

6. Children, Our Greatest Teachers

A few of my stories of the priceless wisdom I was gifted from my children follow:

Always do your personal best. This was a lesson I learned from Luke. He sent me the following text after completing his sophomore year at ASU:

WOW, somehow, I ended up getting a 100% on my accounting final, giving me an A+ in the class. So, I'm ending with 5 A's and one A+ in my hardest class. I technically got two other A+'s but those specific teachers don't give out + and - .

My reply to his text message: You're the best top" A" business student at ASU Luke! So, putting up with that liberal accounting teacher, working hard all semester, and your final double hard focus on exams delivered a 100% on the final and an A+ In Accounting. And all A's across the board. Way to go our fine young man. Follow your big dreams and focus on your immediate goals. Life is a daring adventure or nothing at all. Thank you, Luke, for teaching me so many wonderful things. Especially how much I can love my son. I love you Luke!! Dad 😊

A second valuable lesson I earned from Luke is the power of verbal and body communication when working with our sport teams. In High School, Luke became a member of a new paintball team that was training for a tournament. I asked him how it was going. He said they will soon be going to tournaments and they were working on the hardest part of what they were failing to do: good COMMUNICATION on the fighting fields. I shared with him that good communication is the most important value we have as we strive to be successful in all our experiences. He agreed.

One day Luke came home from grade school and shared a saying he put in writing from that day: "make sure the movie you are making is one that you want to watch when you grow old". What a great lesson from my 10-year-old to me.

Cody once shared a story with me about the importance of dreaming BIG. He was applying at Veterinary Schools in Europe where he was accepted at the University of London, the University of Glasgow and the University of Edenborough. When he received his letter of acceptance at the University of Glasgow, he sent me a copy of the acceptance email with his simple message, "I did it".

We decided to go visit all three universities in Europe to help Cody decide which university to attend. On the train from Glasgow, to Edenborough, he was struggling with his decision. It was only then he shared with me that when he was in fourth grade, he had asked his teacher, Mr. Hart, where and who had the best Veterinary School in the world.

After some research, Mr. Hart shared with Cody that per the rankings he studied, the best Veterinarian school in the world was the University of Glasgow. I was shocked and honored to learn that Cody had been following his BIG DREAM since fourth Grade to attend Glasgow. And that explained to me why, as now a Senior in High School, Cody simply said "I did it" when he received his acceptance letter from Glasgow. Wow…talk about dreaming big, and making your dreams come true! He did work hard, having received straight A's through his schooling to achieve his dream. And taught me the lesson to always dream BIG!

Then there was the Cody EXPERIENCE I had while skiing with my three sons in Deer Valley. I learned about teamwork and being of service from my three sons. One beautiful winter day we were all skiing Lady Morgan, an expert rated hill at Deer Valley.

Together we skied the double black diamond run called Centennial. About two thirds of the way down my speed built up and was forced to ski between two huge pine trees which were very close together. One of my ski poles got snagged between the two trees and was ripped out of my hand. Fortunately, my glove slipped off with the pole versus my hand being broken. My pole was found buried in the snow, bent at a right angle with by empty glove hanging off it. My son Cody had my back, helped me out of the snow drift I was buried in, then lent me his ski poles. He then followed me the rest of the way down the mountain to safety. A true lesson in gifting and teamwork.

One day, Troy taught me a huge lesson in how to relax, not worry and "live in the moment". After much work, focus and dedication attending flight school on his free time, Troy was awarded his private pilot's license. This, while still attending ASU full time and being a member of the Arizona National Guard. I will never forget his first solo flight and much to my relief, landing safely. A week after, he asked if I was willing to be his first passenger after just being awarded his new license. Of course, I was willing and able and ready to go.

As Troy went through his pre-flight check list and revved up the engine on our small single engine Cessna aircraft, the whole plane began vibrating and shaking. Becoming very nervous, I turned and watched Troy as he scanned the controls, pushed / pulled buttons, talked on the radio, scanned around and stepped on the rudders. He was doing all this while at the same time talking on the radio with the Tower getting approval to taxi to the runway. At that moment in time, I witnessed his self-confidence and complete "in control" of the situation. Talk about SITUATIONAL AWARENESS kicking in.

I suddenly relaxed, and felt the most serenity, calmness and peace I have ever felt in my life. I completely trusted and respected Troy, and that returned me to love. Troy was teaching me, by his ACTIONS, truly how it felt for me to "live in the moment" and be at peace. This was a wonderful EXPERIENCE for me in how we always have a choice between LOVE or FEAR.

This is another of many Troy Lessons affirmed to me as a gift from a previous "dad quote' I had shared with Troy. While attending ASU, Troy's assignment one day was to share a quote that he had heard in the past that's helped him through challenges in life. Troy told me he shared and discussed a quote which I had shared with him in the past: "fast is slow and slow is fast". He shared with the class that saying has helped him with his flying lessons and to always take his time while working through life's challenging experiences.

Troy also helped me to remember that we will Manifest what we think!

Troy shared with me one day that he was having serious self-doubts about all the things he was trying to accomplish. This included attending ASU, working on his degree in Engineering, taking flying lessons, and at the same time serving in the Air National Guard as a crew chief on a KC 140 Ariel Refueler.

I acknowledged his feelings and said to try and stay focused on living in the moment and always doing his personal best. Self-doubt is fear trying to take control. Remain self-confident and THINK POSITIVE as we always manifest what we think. Lessons learned for us all!

Finally, a great gift to me from raising my children was The Five Love Languages authored by Gary Chapman. After reading and studying his book, I was now AWARE of how powerful our Love Languages are in how we built and prosper in our relationships with our children, spouses, friends, and associates at work. I also ended up teaching short courses at MSI on the Five Love Languages which follow:

The Five Love Languages

1) **Physical Touch**: Some of us love to be hugged and touched, others not so much.

2) **Words of Affirmation**: Some need many "atta boys" and words of praise each day to keep going, others motive themselves with their own thoughts.

3) **Quality Time:** Time is a very valuable commodity to us all. Some of our close relationships require a lot of our personal time to be happy, and others not as much

4) **Gifts:** The surprise gift is a big motivator to some. To others they can "take it or leave it" and move on with their own inspirations.

5) **Acts of Service:** Many love it when we do "surprise things" for them to help them out with their daily lives. Others would just a soon do it themselves and know it was done "their way".

We all have a blend of the above Five Love Languages that help us be happy and enjoy life with our loved ones.

7. Greatest Gifts

The following are the Greatest Gifts I've learned from my children:

Feeling your feelings
Self esteem
Compassion
Balance
Humor
Communication
Abundance
Integrity, respect and trust

Conscious Choice and the Power of FOCUS. I have been asked at times, "how I was able to raise such good kids and still keep my company flourishing?" My answer is always the same and said with confidence: "Give them your unconditional love and spend plenty of quality time with them." Learn to balance family life with business while being a good leader at your company and a good partner for your spouse.

Follow my following formula 3 + 4 + 3 = 10. This will help guide you on how to be a TEN when it comes to being an entrepreneur while spending time and unconditional love with your family.

3) Life's Journey:

- Relationships
- Experience
- Education

4) Life's Values:

- Impeccable integrity
- Never assume

- Don't take things personally (live in the moment, think positive and love life)

3) Leadership in Life:

- Communication
- Honesty / Truth / Integrity
- Positivity / Peace / Love

My gifted Lesson Learned: You are at peace and happy when everything in your world including people, places and things, are perceived and accepted to be exactly as they are.

My true belief: Gratitude is the secret to happiness!

Always do your personal best. Trust, Respect and always be in your Integrity with your family and associates.

I believe our greatest teachers are our children, our employees and our customers. The answer to the question can you run a company as an entrepreneur and still raise a successful family? I must first share I am so very grateful for all I have learned from my children. They have been the best teachers in my life. YES, being an entrepreneur and being blessed with a wonderful family are both possible-together.

In summary how do we successfully balance Family, Life and Business?

First you must believe in delegation. With delegation comes trust and trust brings solid, loving relationships. In order to delegate effectively you must first learn how. This begins with learning and experiencing accountability....and being responsible for your actions. You learn by experience...like I did in the military and with

Hyatt. I believe that Leadership / delegation are virtues learned through experience only.

Once you've experienced how to effectively delegate and hold people accountable the next step is creating a set of guiding principles which set the values of your organization. Then, a mission statement which sets the strategic direction of your team. Next, you must have clearly defined company goals, then departmental goals and individual employee goals which support the mission statement and company goals.

Next comes clearly defined employee conduct values / guidelines. Once this is accomplished, focused meetings must be held to keep those you delegated to accountable and on track with your goals.

Follow up in writing with messages which are used for clarity, focus and consolidated team vision. "People, product and focus with a passion for excellence." This was MSI 3's tag line I used at the end of my signature block. It's our emotions that drive us to buy, sell, and be proactive. We only act when our emotions kick in, both good and bad. If we take care of our family and people, our employees will take care of our customers.

We must make sure we are emotionally attached to our people, so we are truly understanding their personal problems and challenges. Gallup surveys help to insure all employees are staying on course and have the tools they need to be successful. A good servant leader and family man is always discussing, coaching, and demonstrating good values. The key is to focus on our values including integrity, honesty, courage, trust, leadership, fellowship, empathy and humility.

Chapter Seventeen

Epilogue

After all these BUSINESS, FAMILY and LIFE experiences, I am most blessed to have a family to love and take care of. Connie, Troy, Cody, Luke, Rachael, Alanna, Cory, Kaylee, (with two baby girls) and I all live happily in Arizona. Connie's Birth daughter, Jenny, lives in the Bay Area with her husband and their young son and daughter, making us grandparents times four.

And, after another year of battling cancer, this time including major surgery, months of chemo treatments, (which again put me in the hospital for many weeks) and a long period of physical recovery, I have again been declared cancer free. ☺

Appendix

MSI Performance Review and Process Checklist

- Request a copy of last year's the RF (Review Form) from HR
- Complete SRF (Salary Request Form) and submit to HR for approval
- Schedule the review and provide a blank copy of the RF to associate for a "self-review" one week prior to review.
- Complete Review Form
- See associate, obtain copy of the "self-review" and provide associate with a copy of the competed review form one day prior to review.
- Conduct the review, review last year's goals and agree to and list next year's goals.
- Sign and provide the associate a completed copy of the review
- Provide HR the original copy of the RF and SRF for personnel file

MSI PERFORMANCE REVIEW

Performance Review for:

Title/Department:

Reviewed by:

Review Period:

The MSI Performance Appraisal is a participative process designed to align your individual goals and position description with the companies guiding principles and goals. The following Guiding Principles are used as a point of reference during our meeting.

REVIEW RATINGS:

1 = *Unsatisfactory* - Does not perform required tasks; requires constant supervision.

2 = *Needs Improvement* - Needs improvement in quality of work; completes tasks, but not on time.

3 = *Meets Standards and Expectations* - Meets requirements. Tasks are completed on time.

4 = *Exceeds Standards and Expectations* - Goes above and beyond expectations.

5 = *Clearly Outstanding* - Always gets results far beyond what is required.

Position Description & Responsibilities (see attached description):

	1	2	3	4	5	n/a
I understand my position description and it fits my responsibilities	☐	☐	☐	☐	☐	☐
I enjoy what I do at MSI	☐	☐	☐	☐	☐	☐

COMMENTS: _____

Quality

	1	2	3	4	5	n/a
Knowledge of position and related responsibility	☐	☐	☐	☐	☐	☐
Production of high-quality results	☐	☐	☐	☐	☐	☐
Ability to understand new material and concepts	☐	☐	☐	☐	☐	☐
Understands and achieves individual and company goals	☐					☐

COMMENTS: _____

Production and Organization Skills

	1	2	3	4	5	n/a
Level of productivity	☐	☐	☐	☐	☐	☐
Ability to keep "work in process" well organized	☐	☐	☐	☐	☐	☐
Recognizes potential problems and develops solutions	☐	☐	☐	☐	☐	☐

Area of responsibility is clean and orderly

☐ ☐ ☐ ☐ ☐ ☐

COMMENTS: _____

Integrity – Trust, Respect, Fairness

	1	2	3	4	5	n/a
Honors commitments to internal and external clients	☐	☐	☐	☐	☐	☐
Takes responsibility for actions	☐	☐	☐	☐	☐	☐
Dependability and attendance	☐	☐	☐	☐	☐	☐
Is respected and trusted by co-workers	☐	☐	☐	☐	☐	☐
Makes others feel important and appreciated	☐	☐	☐	☐	☐	☐

COMMENTS: _____

Effective Communication

	1	2	3	4	5	n/a
Actively listens, effectively communicates	☐	☐	☐	☐	☐	☐
Ability to communicate in writing	☐	☐	☐	☐	☐	☐
Communication is open and honest	☐	☐	☐	☐	☐	☐
Offers constructive suggestions for improvement	☐	☐	☐	☐	☐	☐

Helpful and courteous to internal and external clients

☐ ☐ ☐ ☐ ☐

COMMENTS: _____

Leadership

	1	2	3	4	5	n/a
Ability to supervise and motivate staff	☐	☐	☐	☐	☐	☐
Self-motivation and initiative	☐	☐	☐	☐	☐	☐
Leads by example and with empathy	☐	☐	☐	☐	☐	☐
Open to constructive feedback, does not take things personally	☐	☐	☐	☐	☐	☐

COMMENTS: _____

Service – Community, Associates, Customers

	1	2	3	4	5	n/a
Teamwork	☐	☐	☐	☐	☐	☐
Supports and helps others whenever possible	☐	☐	☐	☐	☐	☐
Participates in company charitable based events	☐	☐	☐	☐	☐	☐

COMMENTS: _____

Overall Performance Rating

☐ ☐ ☐ ☐ ☐

Five Goals and/or Achievements from previous Year:

Met   Not Met

☐ ☐

1. _____

☐ ☐

2. _____

☐ ☐

3. _____

☐ ☐

4. _____

☐ ☐

5. _____

Goals and/or Achievements planned for this year:

1. _____

2. _____

3. _____

4. _____

5. _____

Comments from Manager

Comments from Associate:

MSI GALLUP SURVEY

Employee Name: Date:

		Y/N
1	Do I know what is expected of me at work?	
2	Do I have the materials and equipment I need to do my work right?	
3	At work, do I have the opportunity to do what I do best every day?	
4	In the last seven days, have I received recognition or praise for good work?	
5	Does my supervisor, or someone at work, seem to care about me as a person?	
6	Is there someone at work who encourages my development?	
7	At work, do my opinions seem to count?	
8	Does the mission/purpose of my company make me feel like my work is important?	
9	Are my co-workers committed to doing quality work?	
10	Do I have a best friend at work (Is there someone I can confide in)?	

| 11 | In the last six months, have I talked with someone about my progress? | |
| 12 | At work, have I had opportunities to learn and grow? | |

MSI Position / Job Description

Title: **VP of Product Development and Cloud Services**

Department: Product Development

Reports To: CEO

Position Description: Responsible for the development efforts of the Product Development and Cloud Services teams in Phoenix, AZ.

Responsibilities

- Works with the PDG management team to set product and technology direction for MSI.
- Direct and manage development staff in the quality and professional delivery of applications reviewing results on an ongoing basis and giving input for future performance.
- Represent MSI development efforts and direction with partners, vendors and customers.
- Responsible for the direction, monitoring, and appraising the performance of the development team members, providing input to training needs, for new and upgraded products, development of the team, and recommended effective personnel action.
- Ensure smooth execution of Software Development Life Cycle (SDLC).
- Coordinate and work with departments outside of PDG to ensure integration into all MSI department activities and goals.
- Consults with development team to ensure tools and methods of sound practices are used in all development efforts.
- As part of the Product Development Group, it is everyone's responsibility to increase the quality of our products through management of testing and release processes.
- Participate in the education of product direction, standards, and philosophies of development practices as established by the PDG Management team and Product team.

- Provides strong leadership to achieve an overall improvement in performance, based on mutually determined goals, and assist in managing to lower and or contain costs.
- Partners with other management members to improve service quality and improve customer satisfaction.
- Works with Product team to create and maintain MSI solutions roadmap to ensure MSI products and services continue to evolve and maintain MSI as a "Solutions Provider" leader in the hospitality industry.
- Architect and innovate products and solutions to meet customer and market needs.
- Develop and maintain guidelines, patterns, and policies to be used in systems, products, and services.
- Monitor technology trends and developments in the software industry.
- Participate in technology groups as needed.
- Provide day to day leadership and direction to Development Mangers, Product Managers, CST Manager, and IT Administrator.
- Plan and execute technology initiatives for decreased expense and optimal ROI of MSI operations and services offered.
- Ensure quality of products and services is maintained.
- Ensure SLA service levels are met by all technology systems and services.
- Ensure regulatory compliance is maintained by all internal and external products, services, systems, and internal policies and procedures.
- Provide leadership to ensure MSI is technologically positioned for ongoing success.
- Provide timely and accurate information to support MSI business process.
- Provide technical direction to all departments as needed.
- Builds and executes cloud infrastructure strategy for hosting MSI cloud-based applications and services which maximizes services availability and minimized infrastructure cost and maintenance requirements
- Builds and executes security strategies and policies to ensure security in all information systems including cloud infrastructure
- Communicate and collaborate effectively both inside the organization, and with outside vendors and clients.

- Ensures the utmost level of availability of mission critical software/services & systems available to our client base.
- Provide project & management leadership for the Cloud Services support teams.
- Oversee the 24x7 operation of our Highly Available applications and manage deployment of all major cloud application releases.
- Provide high service level for releases and changes to evolving Dev, QA and Stage and Production environments
- Oversee Cloud Services support team, and provide timely resolution to escalated internal and customer issues
- Develop and implement processes/procedures, ensure that established policies and procedures are followed for consistency across the organization.

Required Skills & Experience

- Bachelor's degree in engineering, business, related field, or equivalent work experience required.
- Ten (10) or more years of demonstrated administration, management or supervisory experience required.
- Must be self-motivated, dynamic, creative team player, yet be able to work on own initiative.
- Must be able to effectively manage multiple projects simultaneously.
- Must possess a strong sense of urgency for goal achievement.
- Must possess excellent organizational, analytical, communications, problem solving and decision-making, and policy development & implementation skills.

About the Author

Rick Munson, Founder and past President and CEO of Multi-Systems, Inc., (MSI), founded MSI in 1990 when he purchased International Property Control Systems Inc. (IPCS) from HFS Incorporated. Since then, he dedicated his career to building MSI into a hospitality industry technology leader. The company grew under Munson's leadership to over 200 employees and 6500 hotel installations throughout the Americas.

MSI's growth and success was fueled over the years through the purchase of NovaPLUS from Pegasus and REMco Software Inc from McNeill Associates. With headquarters in Phoenix, AZ, MSI boasted a list of management companies and hotel chains that included Hyatt's Hyatt Place properties, LaQuinta, Best Western, Extended Stay America, Wyndham's Hawthorne brand, Value Place, and more.

Prior to founding MSI, Rick served as Vice President, Sales & Marketing, at IPCS. In that role, he was responsible for the successful development and implementation of the industry's first integrated Central Reservation / Property Management & Sales and Catering solution for Ramada hotels. As the company's primary development officer, Rick more than doubled the size of IPCS's customer base and increased revenues by more than 100% in less than three years.

Before joining IPCS, Rick held strategic positions in sales, marketing, and operations in the hotel industry, including six years as Director of Catering and Convention Services at the Hyatt Regency, Phoenix.

As a graduate of the University of Wyoming, he received a degree in business administration with honors as a Distinguished Military Graduate. Following his graduation, he served as First Lieutenant with key leadership positions as a Platoon Leader and Troop Executive Officer in the highly select Third Armored Cavalry Regiment, Fort Bliss, Texas. Rick received the Meritorious Service Award and other honors for his five years of service to our country.

MSI's Guiding Principles were created by Rick over 15 years ago. With guidance from the MSI team, these Principles were updated and enhanced over the years. Today, they stand as a lighthouse, guiding the MSI team as they reached out in service and gratitude to fellow associates and customers.

Rick is devoted to numerous civic and charitable causes in the Phoenix area. This includes being named \ Co-President of the Kiva PTO, Founder and President of the Kiva Dads Club, Board Member and Secretary of the Phoenix Crisis Nursery, President of Cheney HOA, and past Coach / Coordinator for the ASUSC Soccer. Rick resides happily in Paradise Valley with his wife and eight children.

A FEW FAVORITES
Being a Dad
Coaching Kids
Teaching / Learning Values & Spirituality
Snow Skiing / Hiking / Boating / Travel
Oceans, Forests, Sunsets, and Christmas

IN A WORD
Grateful

www.ingramcontent.com/pod-product-compliance
Lightning Source LLC
Chambersburg PA
CBHW021002180526
45163CB00005B/1864